T0114373

PERFORM!

The Illustrated Thoughts

Toh Tiong Yau

 www.trafford.com

Introduction

"Perform! *The illustrated thoughts*" is a collection of illustrations that depicts the ideas of performance. However these illustrations are not just picture representation of the ideas. Rather, there are different ideas and deeper meaning that can be drawn when you look at these pictures from multiple angles and let your imagination works freely. By doing so, you can reconsider your understanding towards high performance and take decisions to achieve even greater heights.

The illustrations are inspired by the many discussions that occur in my successful performance management workshops that are delivered for many organizations from different industries across the Asia region since 2005.

For the first 12 months that I discussed the ideas and methods of "Perform! *The illustrated thoughts*" in the workshops through the pictures illustrated in this book, more than 900 managers and executives have attended. Since 2005, more than 15000 persons have received the training. Many self discoveries about performance management were made from these illustrations when they discuss together on their meaning. Today, there is a continuous growing interest among those that I have spoken with to learn more about these ideas and methods and how to use it at work. For this, I have decided to compile these illustrations into this book for your convenience. Whether you are an employee, an employer, a consultant, educator, a volunteer or someone doing your own business, you will find these illustrations useful to ponder over the important ideas and methods of performance.

This book has 3 parts. The first part focuses on the various key ideas of performance. The second part follows a typical discussion on performance management, from planning through to developing the performer. The third part combines all ideas previously shown into 6 factors to uplift our performance. These factors are organized around 3 essential aspects of your mind, behavior and environment.

Eventually while we aim to achieve high performance, we also aim to be happy about our choices and actions. Neither needs to be compromised or attained at the expense of the other. So let us rediscover high performance – happily.

CONTENTS

CONTENTS (continue)

Part 2   Ideas of Performance Management

CONTENTS (continue)

A few words

Performance is highly sought after. High performance is valued even more. The simple reason is that it creates outcomes and impact that are desirable and needed. It is not a fad and it will never go out of fashion. In whatever field; and for generations in the present and future, high performance will always be a state that everyone seeks to attain or celebrate!

And high performance is within our reach. It does not only belong to a special group of privileged or talented people. For as long as you believe in your cause, passionate about your work, decide to engage yourself and dare to try – in short, make aiming for high performance a strong habit, you will succeed.

When you can make high performance a strong habit, you will frequently and consistently bring happiness to self and others. But strong habits do not come by naturally. They are products of hard work and persistent efforts. And often having a start point to regroup your thinking is important as you take this long journey of making good habits permanent.

I hope the illustrations in this book will serve as a stepping board for you to imagine creatively and form your own insights into the true meaning of what excellent performance means to you. And then from here, you can make choices that would realize your performance dreams.

How to use this book?

The illustrations in this book can be used by you with others or by yourself. Below are some examples of how you may use this book.

With others

- Use illustrations as discussion points in a meeting

- Use illustrations to prompt others to think differently or deeper

- Use illustrations to review or revise your team goals and work objectives

- Use illustrations to brainstorm new ideas on performance not thought of previously

- Use illustrations to coach & explain to others on performance management

With self (alone)

- Use illustrations to reflect on own performance thinking

- Use illustrations to consider own performance plans further (where to change or improve)

- Use illustrations to reaffirm why I am doing it

- Use illustrations to teach self on performance management

- Use illustrations to deepen own thoughts about performance management

For each illustration, there are notes that may provide some perspectives on its meaning. In addition, there are also 3 questions accompanying each illustration for you to ponder. You may use the notes and questions to jump start your reflection or discussions. Alternatively, you can look at the illustrations and consider directly for their meaning and significance.

Perform! *The illustrated thoughts* by Toh Tiong Yau

Key Ideas of High Performance

Key Ideas of High Performance

The 10 key ideas of high performance are common areas of discussions on performance

A starting point to appreciate the idea of high performance is to compare basic performance and performance so that you can recognize their importance and purpose in your mission to work. The 3 ideas here are:

- Basic performance & performance
- Nature of performance
- Nature of basic performance

Whether it is basic performance or performance, they contain both aspects of results and efforts that you will show. The idea is to recognize their impact on you as a performer so that you will not lose sight of high desirable efforts as you attain high results. The 3 ideas here are:

- Results & efforts
- Impact of results & efforts
- Results & efforts – relationships

Seeing the ideas of performance at work is to follow it through the stages of planning, tracking and appraising, commonly found in organizations. Each of these stages has its purpose. Collectively, they form the platform for continuous performance. The 3 ideas here are:

- 3 stages of performance management
- 3 stages – outcome, time, focus
- Spiral of PTA

Lastly, the WIIFM (what's in it for me) for performance is a recurring question if it is not answered adequately and properly. This is because the performer may not be fully committed to excel when there is doubt that whatever is contributed will not be recognized or rewarded as expected. If this happens, then you would be distracted from giving your best because you are not convinced that you will receive the best in return. On the other hand, it is a booster to high performance if this question is answered well. The idea here is:

- Return on performance (R.O.P.)

BASIC PERFORMANCE & PERFORMANCE

"Pasture"

Like a pasture, "Performance" will
grow, change & develop

"Concrete"

Like a concrete wall, "Basic Performance"
aims for stability & predictability

Notes:

In a broad sense, performance is about attaining desired results. For this, we can look at it in 2 ways:

	Basic performance	Performance
What :	Day-to-day activities	Growth, change or development activities
Where :	Work responsibilities	Work objectives & projects

QUESTIONS TO PONDER:

1. Can you achieve performance but fail in basic performance?
2. How much will it matter if you achieve basic performance, but not performance?
3. What would happen when basic performance and performance are not linked?

NATURE OF PERFORMANCE

Like a clouds, "Performance" is dynamic, temporary, open to change & has a rising tendency.

"Clouds"

Notes:
As performance implies growth, change and/or development, it has certain differentiating characteristics:

	Characteristics of performance
State	: Dynamic
Effect	: Temporary (changing)
Tendency	: Rising
Attitude	: Open to change

QUESTIONS TO PONDER:
1. How would performance arise from basic performance?
2. In what ways would performance be needed if basic performance is excellent already?
3. How would performance be sustainable if basic performance is not done properly?

NATURE OF BASIC PERFORMANCE

Like sky, "Basic Performance" is stable & permanent,
changes gradually & reaches out

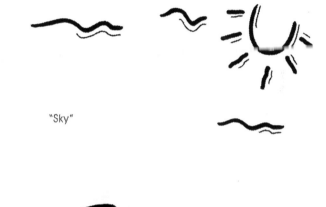

"Sky"

Notes:
As basic performance implies day-to-day work activities, it has certain calming characteristics:

Characteristics of basic performance

State	: Stable
Effect	: Permanent (predictable)
Tendency	: Gradual improvement
Attitude	: Resistant to change

QUESTIONS TO PONDER:

1. How would basic performance give rise to performance?
2. How possible is it when basic performance breaks down and yet you attain performance?
3. When and how would performance become basic performance?

RESULTS & EFFORTS

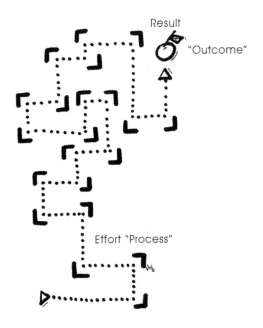

Notes:

Whether it is basic performance or performance, there are 2 aspects that cannot be compromised:

	Results	Efforts
What	: Seen as outcomes	Seen as behaviors
Influence	: The efforts	The results
Know	: Survival status(e.g. pass or fail)	Survival instinct (e.g. going to pass or fail)

QUESTIONS TO PONDER:
1. How would results give meaning to efforts?
2. How would efforts alter the aim of results?
3. What are the consequences when results and efforts are not balanced?

IMPACT OF RESULTS & EFFORTS

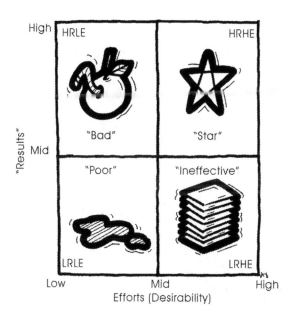

Notes:
The combined effects of "Result" & "Desirable Effort" can create a performer:

High result / high (desirable) effort   : Star performers
Low result / high (desirable) effort   : Ineffective performers
High result / low (desirable) effort   : Bad performers
Low result / high (desirable) effort   : Poor performers

QUESTIONS TO PONDER:
1. What would happen in the longer term if you focus only on results?
2. What would happen in the longer term if you focus only on desirable efforts?
3. How to promote high results & high desirable efforts at the same time?

RESULTS & EFFORTS – RELATIONSHIPS

"Chain" - Correlation

Move one end
the other may move

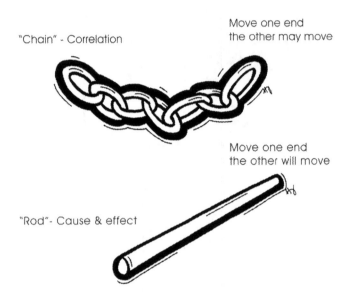

Move one end
the other will move

"Rod"- Cause & effect

Notes:
The benefit of seeing result & effort together is that you can manage either before it is too late:

Results & (desirable) Efforts
... are correlated   : Other factors need to be addressed
... are related by cause & effect : Other factors are secondary

3 STAGES OF PERFORMANCE MANAGEMENT

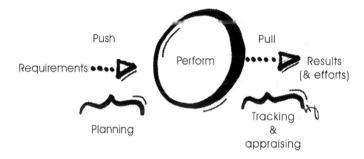

Notes:

Performance won't happen automatically, it arises when you "push" it out, and then "pull" it continuously:

Push performance : Requirements *i.e. planning*
Pull performance : Results & efforts *i.e. tracking & appraising*

QUESTIONS TO PONDER:
1. What if planning is weak... or strong?
2. What if tracking is weak... or strong?
3. What if appraising is weak... or strong?

3 STAGES – OUTCOME, TIME, FOCUS

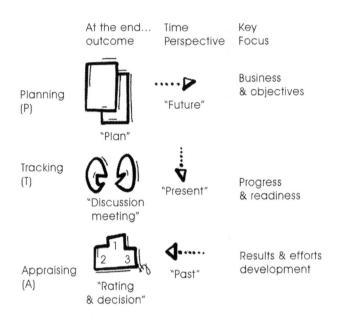

	At the end... outcome	Time Perspective	Key Focus
Planning (P)	"Plan"	"Future"	Business & objectives
Tracking (T)	"Discussion meeting"	"Present"	Progress & readiness
Appraising (A)	"Rating & decision"	"Past"	Results & efforts development

Notes:
Be familiar with each stage of performance management will empower you to act decisively & effectively:

	Outcome	Time	Focus
Planning	: Performance plan	Mainly future	Business & objectives
Tracking	: Discussion meeting	Mainly present	Progress & readiness
Appraising	: Ratings & decisions	Mainly past	Results, efforts & development

QUESTIONS TO PONDER:
1. How does planning affect tracking & appraising?
2. How does tracking affect planning & appraising?
3. How does appraising affect planning & tracking?

Perform! *The illustrated thoughts* by Toh Tiong Yau

SPIRAL OF PTA

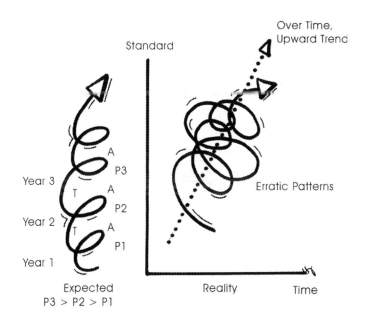

Standard

Over Time,
Upward Trend

Erratic Patterns

Year 3

P3
A
T
A
P2
T
A
P1

Year 2

Year 1

Expected
P3 > P2 > P1

Reality

Time

Notes:
Growth, change & development always imply a spiral upward trend in performance management:

	Benefit
Power of planning	: Break the limit – gain competitive edge
Power of tracking	: Put plan on track
Power of appraising	: Get ready to break next new limit

QUESTIONS TO PONDER:
1. How much do you plan for basic performance or performance?
2. How can you track for progress and readiness?
3. How can appraisals motivate you to score higher next time?

RETURN ON PERFORMANCE
(R.O.P)

"$"

"Career,
learning & reputation"

Performance = $ + career + learning + reputation

Notes:
What you get in return for your performance is dependent on what you give in the first place:

Performance gains:	Attributed to:	Effect:
$	Results	Shorter term (e.g. a year)
Career	Efforts (desirable)	Longer term (e.g. a decade)
Learning	Efforts (desirable)	Longer term (e.g. a decade)
Reputation	Efforts (desirable)	Longer term (e.g. a decade)

QUESTIONS TO PONDER:
1. To what extent is focusing on $ a short term view of your career?
2. What are good yardsticks for indicating your success at work?
3. How would the above performance gains be realized simultaneously?

Realizing Performance Reality

Realizing Performance Reality

In making sense of performance, it is useful to look at the performers, their intentions and the environment that they work in simultaneously as a whole, rather than separate things.

The key is to recognize how the performers form their intention to excel, demonstrate their expertise and interact with their work environment. If you take the performers and their environment separately and deal with them as though one would automatically fit into the other, when you piece them together again, you would go against the natural state of affair.

You can study, design and implement solutions to correct performers or their environment faults independently. But when come to practice in reality, they are intertwined. By your decision, you can implement systems or study performer's behaviors separately. But in consequence, you are correcting the parts instead of the whole performance challenge.

Therefore, it is useful that you maintain a perspective (or attitude) to see the challenges of performance management as 3 inter-dependent forces namely 1) performers' motivations seen through their intentions, 2) their potentials to excel, and 3) the conditions that they operate in, as one single case rather than separate cases. As a breakdown, you can classify performers' motivation (M) as things like their missions, directions, goals, objectives and targets that they want to achieve. Their potentials (P) would include their technical know-how and behavioral competencies. The conditions (C) would be their working environment in terms of work styles that they are subjected to conform (e.g. practices at work), standards (e.g. policies & guidelines) and resources (e.g. money, equipment & time).

Any problems encountered in one of these 3 performance areas, e.g. unclear targets – motivation, lack of skills – potentials or lack of resources – conditions, would affect the state of performance balance. This means the quality and standards of performance outcomes, and morale or commitment of performers would be affected.

The 5 ideas here are:

- MPC factors (factors affecting performance)
- The motivation (mind) factors
- The potentials (person) factors
- The condition (environment) factors
- MPC applications

Perform! *The illustrated thoughts* by Toh Tiong Yau

MPC FACTORS
(FACTORS AFFECTING PERFORMANCE)

"Motivation"
mind factors

Release

Interprets

Acquire

Shape

Activate

Adjust

"Potentials"
person factors

"Conditions"
external factors

Mind shapes the person, acquire the conditions
Person interprets the mind, activate the conditions
Conditions release the minds, adjust the person

Notes:
There is no single factor that creates performance success, it is a combination of 3 groups of factors:

Factors affecting performance

Motivation factors (M) : Goals, objectives, targets

Potentials factors (P) : Technical expertise, behavioral strengths, personal interests & beliefs

Conditions factors (C) : Policies & guidelines, facilities & tools, cultures (how we do things here)

QUESTIONS TO PONDER:
1. Is your M realistic, P ready and C relevant?
2. What are the consequences if one of this factor groups is weak or lacking?
3. What happens if M expires?

THE MOTIVATION FACTORS
(MIND)

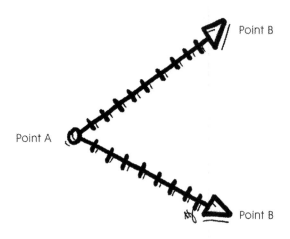

Point B

Point A

Point B

Realistic?

Notes:
The soul of your performance plan starts with what you think:

Motivation (M)
can be seen as

Goal	: A desired end state with timeframe
Objective	: A more specific way to achieve the goal
Target	: A measure of success of the objective

QUESTIONS TO PONDER:
1. How would your M affect the way you use your expertise & competencies at work?
2. To what extend would you hold on to your M in times of adversity?
3. What happens if you have the "wrong" M?

THE POTENTIALS FACTORS
(PERSON)

Knowledge
attitude

Interest

Skills

Ready?

Notes:
The reality of your chances of success depends on you and how well you can access other experts:

Potentials (P)
can be seen as
Technical expertise : Technical or functional knowledge & skills
Behavioral strengths : Thinking, communicating & social skills
Personal interests & beliefs : Attitude & values

QUESTIONS TO PONDER:
1. To what extent is all those people with strong P are also high performers?
2. To what extent can you acquire P?
3. To what extent can other's P be engaged for your own causes?

THE CONDITION FACTORS
(ENVIRONMENT)

The External Factors

Relevant?

Notes:
There is no way you can detach yourself from where you need to get results from:

Conditions (C)
can be seen as
Policies & guidelines   : Dos & don'ts / operating procedures
Facilities & tools   : Infrastructure & hardware to operate work
Cultures (how we do things here) : Social & work styles

QUESTIONS TO PONDER:
1. To what extent is C man-made?
2. When C limits your efforts, what else can you do?
3. How to change the C given to you?

MPC APPLICATIONS

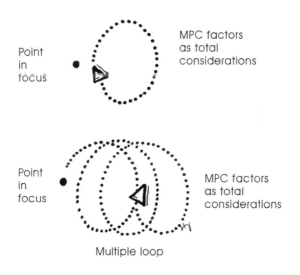

Point
in
focus

MPC factors
as total
considerations

Point
in
focus

MPC factors
as total
considerations

Multiple loop

Notes:
M, P & C factors can be used to manage performance – decision making, problem definition, solution selection, making plans, changing courses or motivating others:

Loop Steps
Define   : The point in focus, e.g. a problem, a concern, an issue
Seek out : M, P & C factors that resolve the point in focus (obvious & not so obvious ones)
Decide   : The best combination of factors that can start as next steps forward

QUESTIONS TO PONDER:
1. Where is their link between factors when M, P & C factors are considered together?
2. When seeking "solutions" for "problem", to what extent would emphasizing M (solutions) for M (problem), P (solutions) for P (problem) & C (solutions) for C (problem) approach work?
3. Having decided on solutions for now, will they be still so later in the future?

Seeking Performance Success

Seeking Performance Success

To be successful in your business, you will want to offer solutions that your customers want or need. To do so, you will want to ensure that your work is effective in creating the solutions and that you have good partners to help you achieve more than you can. But your customers always have choices. So you will also need to keep a competitive edge over your competitors in order to stay ahead or remain in the game.

The above ideas can be arranged into 6 areas, link up into 3 parts of consideration. You can match your solutions & customers, combine your work with your partners and stake your competencies with your competitors.

The 7 ideas here are:

- (Core) business success factors
- Key customers – needs
- Key partners – focus
- Key competitors – challenges
- Core solutions – relevance
- Core work – simplicity
- Core competencies – edge

BUSINESS SUCCESS FACTORS

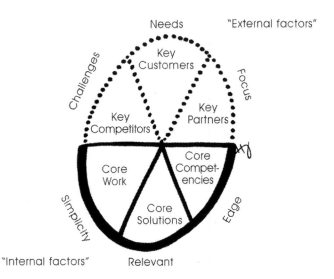

Notes:
Clear about what will make you successful is one thing, able to match them up will make a difference:

Customers & solutions : Basically, needs are met
Competitors & competencies : Have an edge over challenges
Partners & work : Clear focus that is simple to work out

QUESTIONS TO PONDER:
1. How to balance external demands (customers / competitors / partners) with internal capabilities (solutions / competencies / core work)?
2. Where there is an area of weakness, will there be another area of strength to compensate?
3. How can you turn a loss to a gain?

KEY CUSTOMERS – NEEDS

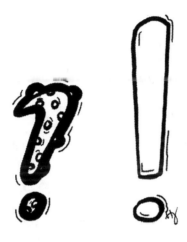

Have answers to their questions?

Notes:

Customer is the first person you must think of, he is also the last person you cannot forget:

Customer's needs

Expected	: Basic, essential or required
Unexpected	: Unplanned, surprised or consequential (as a result of)
New	: Improved version, changes or new areas
Not requested (yet)	: Not aware, future needs or desire, trends

QUESTIONS TO PONDER:

1. To what extent can you provide a solution to your customer's needs?
2. In what ways will your customers be better off with you?
3. How long term is your relationships with your customers?

KEY PARTNERS – FOCUS

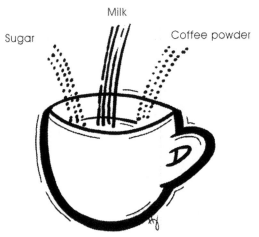

Each has its purposes &
connects well with each other?

Notes:
Business partners exist to make thing happens, make it works and make it better:

Focus of partners

Value chain	: e.g. suppliers / part process owners / franchise / license
Parent-subsidiary	: e.g. HQ / JV / government-linked
Sponsor / investor	: e.g. private investors / public investors / fund provider
Colleagues	: e.g. the person working next to you / your boss & staff

QUESTIONS TO PONDER:
1. What can we do together that we cannot accomplish alone?
2. How well can we work together?
3. How much more duplication or multiple handling can we eliminate?

CORE SOLUTIONS – RELEVANCE

Day & night...
Substainable?

Notes:
If you do not have a business case in the first place, try do something else:

Core solutions

Life span	: Long or short
Renew possibility	: Standard or can be improved
Add on / serial	: Scoped or open ended
Extent of use	: Single use or multiple uses

QUESTIONS TO PONDER:
1. How essential or needed are your solutions?
2. How affordable are your solutions?
3. How can your solutions contribute to society at large, directly or indirectly?

KEY COMPETITORS – CHALLENGES

Cushion the weight?

Notes:

Competitors exist because you did too well or too badly – either way, don't blame them:

Competitor's challenges

Fundamental	: Targeted at our core solutions
Extra	: Targeted at more of the same thing
Re-packaged	: Targeted at new look & ways
Encompassing	: Targeted at all aspects of our core businesses

QUESTIONS TO PONDER:

1. How to soften the impact of your competitor's challenges?
2. How to convert your competitors into your partners?
3. How to co-operate with your competitors?

CORE WORK – SIMPLICITY

Work units

Do they stack up?

Notes:
If the work you created is so complicated, you have just diminished the need for your solutions:

Core work
Necessity   : Real or fake work
Meaningful : Add value to final solution or unnecessary steps & details
Impact   : Accumulative or synergistic to other related work processes

---

QUESTIONS TO PONDER:
1. Is the work simple enough to be understood & carried out by someone?
2. Does your work translate into value?
3. What would you do if you stop doing your current work now?

CORE COMPETENCIES – EDGE

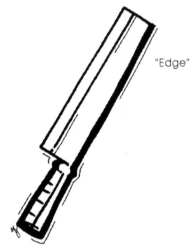

"Edge"

Faster, cheaper, better, easier?

Notes:
Where giving solution for customer is a fundamental idea, your core competencies realize this idea:

Core competencies

Speed	: Do it faster
Cost	: Do it cheaper
Quality	: Do it better
Practicability	: Do it easier

QUESTIONS TO PONDER:
1. What aspects of you & your solutions can be copied or replaced?
2. How important is your originality (e.g. brand) to users or customers?
3. How much confidence can you gain through your core competencies?

Importance & Relevance of Performance Management

Importance & Relevance of Performance Management

Before we get to the details of performance management, it is useful to agree on its importance and relevance.

Performance management is important because it emphasizes the ethical demands on you as a performer. Being mindful of these demands will ensure that you act with conscience and make choices that serve a good cause, or do not go against principles.

Performance management is relevant because high performance needs to be managed. And those who did it need to be rewarded and recognized. If you forget such basic logic, you will find managing performance a chore.

The 3 ideas here are:

- Governance & control
- Productivity & innovation
- Reward & fairness

GOVERNANCE & CONTROL

Support or revolt?

Notes:
Your way of conducting your business will attract similar types of people to buy & do business from you:

Governance : Accountability to stakeholders & public

Control : Code of ethics & conduct

QUESTIONS TO PONDER:
1. Would you want someone to do this to you? Why?
2. Whose support do you want eventually?
3. How can you leave a positive legacy behind?

PRODUCTIVITY & INNOVATION

Alone?

With customers
& competitors?

Notes:
For managers around the world, there are 2 things that are needed year after year:

Productivity   : Give more with the same or lesser resources

Innovation   : Offer different or new things that are valuable

QUESTIONS TO PONDER:
1. To what extent do you work alone?
2. How would other's contributions affect you, and vice versa?
3. How much of your total result is obtained through other's work?

REWARD & FAIRNESS

Physical
hunger

Mental
hunger

Notes:

As an individual performer, managing my performance is important because there are 2 things I want:

Reward   : Monetary, non monetary, tangibles, non tangibles

Fairness : Relative comparison of reward

QUESTIONS TO PONDER:

1. How & why is money important to you?
2. To what extent can "equal reward for all" work?
3. What are the similarities & differences between reward & recognition?

Performance Planning

Performance Planning

Performance planning is the kick off stage of performance management. It is the stage where decisions are made that will shape your actions and outcomes.

Planning is such an essential thing to do for real success to happen. Yet, the irony is that planning can be detached from reality when you approach it purely from a planning point of view, and for too long. The need to ensure that your plan is realistic means that you are continuously matching what is in your mind with what is out there in your real world. You are also taking in what is out there in your real world and create another one in your mind. Either way, it is critical that you remember the reason why you plan in the first place.

To remember the reason why you plan, how you deal with information, define your plan and work with people are activities that will keep you in focus.

The 11 ideas here are:

- 3 aspects of performance planning
- Working with information – unspoken
- Working with information – central focus
- Defining the plan
- Defining the plan – objective
- Defining the plan – GCD
- Defining the plan – why & how
- Defining the plan – stretched targets (types)
- Defining the plan – stretched targets (considerations)
- Working with people – cascade map
- Working with people – line of sight

3 ASPECTS OF PERFORMANCE PLANNING

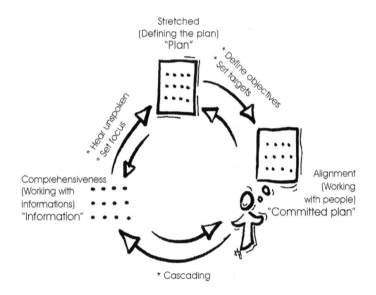

Stretched
(Defining the plan)
"Plan"

* Define objectives
* Set targets

* Hear unspoken
* Set focus

Comprehensiveness
(Working with
informations)
"Information"

Alignment
(Working
with people)
"Committed plan"

* Cascading

Notes:

Performance planning involves 3 aspects of working with information, defining the plan & working with people to gain commitment for the plan. A good plan is formed when the following can be seen:

Performance plan   : What you want to achieve

Quality of plan   : Comprehensive coverage, stretched targets, aligned with others

Success of plan   : Commitment by all involved to give their best

---

QUESTIONS TO PONDER:

1. To what extent do you accept the information given when working out your plan?
2. With regards to your targets, how stretched is stretch enough for you?
3. How well connected should our plan be with others?

WORKING WITH INFORMATION
– UNSPOKEN

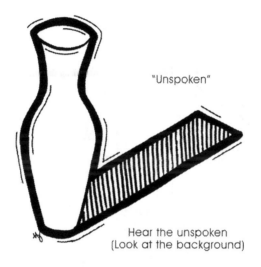

"Unspoken"

Hear the unspoken
(Look at the background)

Notes:
A performance plan is basically formatted information of your intention. Therefore, you need input from others before you can decide where to go and what to accomplish:

Contact points : Information that you come in contact with directly & obviously
(e.g. dialogue, emails, news)

Context points : Background of the information that you come in contact with
(e.g. agenda, intention)

QUESTIONS TO PONDER:
1. Behind every information, how do you spot the purpose that lies beneath?
2. How can you see if what's spoken and speaker's intentions are matched?
3. When conflicting signals are noted, which one do you choose?

WORKING WITH INFORMATION
– CENTRAL FOCUS

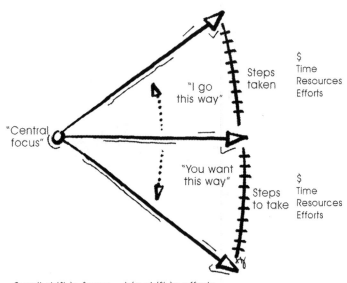

Small shift in focus... big shift in efforts

Notes:
The starting point of your plan is your intention, represented by the focus you choose:

Small shift in focus   : Can lead to big changes in terms of efforts & resources

Small misalignment in focus   : Can lead to unnecessary emphasis on differences

QUESTIONS TO PONDER:
1. When would it be possible for you to shoot first, then aim?
2. By aiming, does it mean you cannot shift your shooting?
3. So what is the purpose of having a focus before you set the details of your plan?

DEFINING THE PLAN

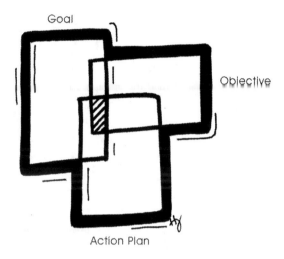

Goal

Objective

Action Plan

"Ideas and points in goal, objective and action plan can be
interchanged, e.g. an action plan idea can be defined
into an objective or goal, vice versa."

Notes:
Your plan must be actionable. But it must be exciting too:

From goal to objective	: Translate dream to targets
From objective to action plan	: Translate targets to action steps
From action plan to goal	: Translate action steps to dream

QUESTIONS TO PONDER:
1. Where can you obtain ideas to form your goal?
2. What do you do if you achieve your objectives, but not your goal?
3. How instinctive should your goal be when you implement your action plans?

DEFINING THE PLAN
– OBJECTIVE

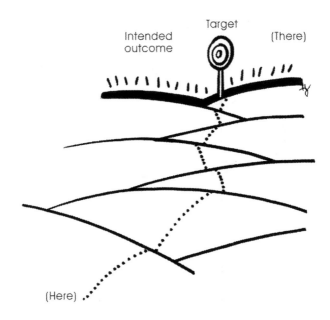

Notes:

Your objective statement has 2 parts that make it whole:

Intention of objective : Intended outcome (I.O.) – what you want to achieve

Success of objective : Target (T) – how you know you are successful

QUESTIONS TO PONDER:
1. What is an objective without a target?
2. How meaningful is a target without an objective?
3. How useful is having objectives in place?

Perform! *The illustrated thoughts* by Toh Tiong Yau

DEFINING THE PLAN
– GCD

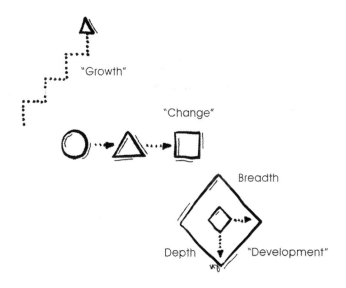

"Growth"

"Change"

Breadth

Depth   "Development"

Notes:
Your focus forms the 3 areas of work for your objectives:

Growth   : To increase profitability, customer base, capacity or capability

Change   : To create new revenue pipelines, new customer groups, new methods or new methods

Development : To improve financial standing (cash flow), customer relations, methods or skills & knowledge

QUESTIONS TO PONDER:
1. In what ways can you expand, increase or acquire (grow)?
2. In what ways can you adopt new or revise old (change)?
3. In what ways can you improve or learn (develop)?

DEFINING THE PLAN
– WHY & HOW

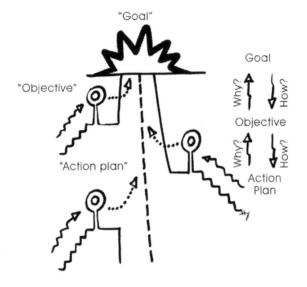

Notes:

To stay committed, relate "Why" to see the link of your objective to your goal and relate "How" to know the steps & methods you will use in your action plan

Why achieve this objective   : To attain the (larger) goal

How to achieve this objective   : To implement the action plan

QUESTIONS TO PONDER:

1. How can you ensure that your action plans add up to achieve your objectives & goals?
2. What can you do when you are not sure why you are achieving your objectives?
3. How much room can you have to change your action plans without derailing from your objectives?

DEFINING THE PLAN
– STRETCHED TARGETS (TYPES)

 "Percentage"   Look at...
                    competing factors

 "Monetary   Look at...
                     value"   value gains

 "Number"   Look at...
                    capacity

"Timing"   Look at...
                    speed efficiency

Notes:
Target is how you measure your success. They can be represented in 4 distinctive ways:

%	: When there are competing factors to manage
$	: When value or gain is to be calculated
#	: When capacity or volume is in focus
Hours & seconds	: When timing must be managed

QUESTIONS TO PONDER:
1. Can everything be measured?
2. How to prevent from being accurately wrong?
3. Do you measure what is necessary?

DEFINING THE PLAN
– STRETCHED TARGETS (CONSIDERATIONS)

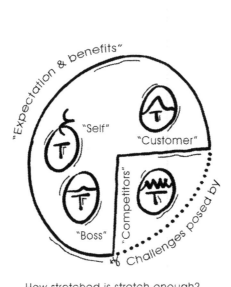

How stretched is stretch enough?

Notes:
"How stretched is stretch enough?"... get the answers from the following people:

Target considerations

Expectations & benefits   : For customers, boss & self

Challenges posed   : By competitors

QUESTIONS TO PONDER:
1. Does your target satisfy your boss & yourself?
2. How long will your target satisfy your customers?
3. Are you competing or defining the competition?

WORKING WITH PEOPLE
– CASCADE MAP

Are we connected?

 "Alignment"

 "Synergy"

 "Composition"

 "Shared"

Notes:
Cascading is about getting people connected with you. They can be connected to you as follow:

Cascade connections

Alignment   : There is hand-over and take-over between us

Synergy   : You cannot help me but your success will impact my output

Composition : We do individual parts but together we make a whole

Shared   : We share the same objectives / targets

QUESTIONS TO PONDER:
1. How can a common goal help us work closer together?
2. What kind of energy will be generated by people working closely together?
3. What challenges do you have to address to get people together?

WORKING WITH PEOPLE
– LINE OF SIGHT

Are we in agreement?

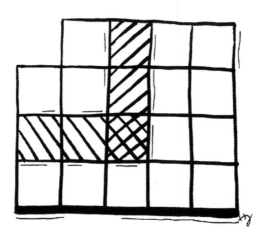

Notes:

Once a connection is established, the clarity of that connection can be seen as follow:

Merge process   : Line of...

Merge point   : Sight

Performance Tracking

Performance Tracking

Performance tracking is the bridge between your plan and your appraisals. Through tracking you will gather evidence on your progress made so far and readiness for the work to be done.

This evidence has two purposes. It serves to tell you now on what adjustments you may need to make to stay on track or perform better. It also serves as points of considerations for appraisals at the end of the performance period.

The key to success is that the evidence obtained through tracking is true and accurate. This is why you must have more than one way to track.

The 5 ideas here are:

- Inspection
- Progress review
- Data used
- Customer feedback
- Discussion meeting

Perform! *The illustrated thoughts* by Toh Tiong Yau

INSPECTION

Completed work - "Accountability"

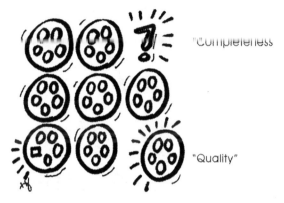

"Completeness"

"Quality"

"Details"

Notes:

Tracking involves collecting performance evidences in terms of the performer's progress for work done, and readiness for work yet to be done. Inspection is a way to see:

Details : Meet all requirements & specifications

Completeness : Nothing is missing

Quality : Nothing is out of order

Accountability : Doing what is supposed to be done

QUESTIONS TO PONDER:

1. What are some of the things that you can inspect easily?
2. What is a good level of involvement with the performer when you inspect?
3. How often should you inspect?

PROGRESS REVIEW

What's done? How well?
What's not yet done? How ready?

Notes:

Tracking involves collecting performance evidences in terms of the performer's progress for work done, and readiness for work yet to be done. Progress review is a way to see:

Capabilities   : Amount of work accomplished so far

Social skills   : Amount of goodwill gained so far

QUESTIONS TO PONDER:

1. How often do you need to conduct progress review?
2. What do you look for in progress reviews?
3. What actions do you take after progress reviews?

DATA USED

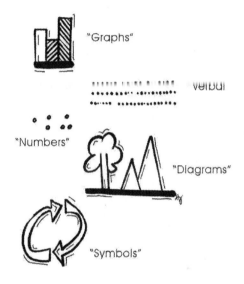

"Graphs"

verbal

"Numbers"

"Diagrams"

"Symbols"

Notes:
Tracking involves collecting performance evidences in terms of the performer's progress for work done, and readiness for work yet to be done. Looking at data used (by performer) is a way to see his:

Interests : Types of information or data worked with

Preferred work styles : Ways of using this information or data

Resourcefulness : Where & who he gets the information or data from

QUESTIONS TO PONDER:
1. Is the person who has the information better than the rest? Why?
2. What happens to those who has the information but are not using them?
3. How can you know the performer better by looking at the data he uses at work?

CUSTOMER FEEDBACK

Notes:
Tracking involves collecting performance evidences in terms of the performer's progress for work done, and readiness for work yet to be done. Customer feedback is a way to see his:

Impact at work   : Satisfied or angry customers

Future potentials : Managing customers

QUESTIONS TO PONDER:
1. In what ways can you speak with your staff's customers directly?
2. In what ways can you ask your customers to see your supervising manager?
3. Where there is conflict between what is said by customers and the performer, what will you do?

DISCUSSION MEETING

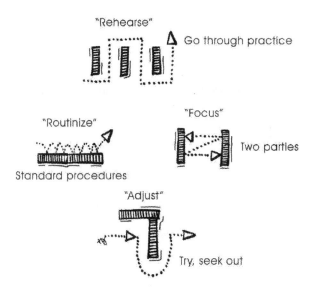

"Rehearse"

Go through practice

"Routinize"

"Focus"

Two parties

Standard procedures

"Adjust"

Try, seek out

Notes:
Having verified tracked evidences with inspection, progress review, data used and customer feedback, a follow-up discussion meeting on performer's progress & readiness is an important wrap-up on tracking. To ensure that such post-tracking meetings are regularly conducted, the following actions are useful:

Rehearse   : Overcome initial reluctance

Focus   : On both performer & you

Adjust   : Duration, time, place, agenda etc.

Routine   : Set as standard procedures

QUESTIONS TO PONDER:
1. How to determine the right frequency of tracking discussion meeting?
2. How formal should these meetings be?
3. Why do you want to conduct tracking discussion meeting?

Performance Appraising

Perform! *The illustrated thoughts* by Toh Tiong Yau

Performance Appraising

Performance appraising is taking stock of performance delivered. The aim is to celebrate what is done well and seek out areas for improvement.

While this aim is simple, the difficulty is that you have to form an opinion that is fair, not too strict or too lenient and consistent with the norm. This art of appraising requires you to practice making appraisal decisions so as to enhance the credibility of your appraisals.

The 4 ideas here are:

- Facts & opinions
- Being fair
- Individual rating – strict or lenient
- Group rating – consistent

FACTS & OPINIONS

Facts   Opinions

Hard   Soft
cold   warm
"Narrative"   "Descriptive"

Notes:
Performance appraisal requires the use of facts and opinions for assessment:

Facts   : There is a place, time, people involved, event happened

Opinions   : What you make out of the above (facts)

QUESTIONS TO PONDER:
1. To what extent do you use facts to form your opinions?
2. Whose opinions will you accept when you appraise?
3. What if the facts and opinions don't quite match up?

BEING FAIR

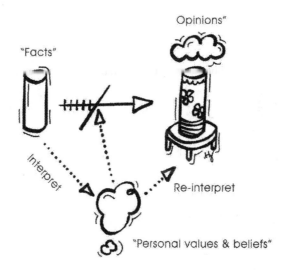

"Opinions"

"Facts"

Interpret

Re-interpret

"Personal values & beliefs"

Notes:
The key to successful performance appraisals is that the performer accepts your assessment & ratings.
Therefore, being seen as a fair appraiser is useful:

Fact-based opinions   : Can be seen as objective & fair

Opinion-based opinions   : Can be seen as subjective & unfair

QUESTIONS TO PONDER:
1. How would your personal beliefs and values affect the way you interpret the facts?
2. How can you verify if your facts are true and accurate?
3. Would my opinions count more than the facts?

INDIVIDUAL RATING
– STRICT OR LENIENT

Strict?

Tight

Relax

Lenient?

Notes:
Performance appraisals will end with ratings & decisions. As an appraiser, your individual ratings become a summary of your opinions of the performance. The thing to know is are you:

Too strict   : Seek 2nd opinions

Too lenient   : Seek more facts

QUESTIONS TO PONDER:
1. How can you practice (trial) performance rating at work?
2. What if the results and desirable efforts don't quite match up?
3. How important is performance rating? Why?

GROUP RATING
– CONSISTENT

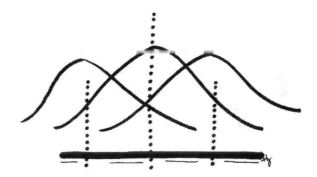

Consistent in progressing?

Notes:
While individual performance rating is an absolute exercise on performance effectiveness, group performance ranking is a relative comparative exercise on who is first and last in the group. Where ratings are ranked into a normal distribution curve, the strategy is to shift the whole curve rightward year on year rather than be too caught up with who's in and who's out of the race:

Consistent   : Result & effort focused

QUESTIONS TO PONDER:
1. How would individual performance rating be useful in deciding learning & development options?
2. How would group performance ranking be useful in distributing rewards & career opportunities?
3. What are possible alternatives if you do not use rating or ranking?

Create Performer's Development

Create Performer's Development

The work of performance management is not complete until the work of developing the performer is done. In fact, such work is of great importance because it puts the human factor back into "management" in performance management.

As people is the force behind performance, the strategic intention of a performer's development plan is to enable him or her to have an edge over competition and a sense of self control & management that leads to high results. This requires you to look beyond weaknesses and tap on every opportunity to raise the overall capabilities of the performer, even if this means redefining work that make his or her weaknesses irrelevant.

The 5 ideas here are:

- Develop strengths
- Eliminate weaknesses
- Career management – toughen up
- Career management – open up
- Career management – grow up

DEVELOP STRENGTHS

Spot the strengthes

Notes:

Strengths can be obvious or they can be subtle and hidden. In any case, strengths are what the performer is already good at. Getting performer to show his strengths is easier than getting him to improve his weaknesses. Therefore it is useful to spot the strengths & develop them further:

	Strengths
Skills	: Can do well
Attitude	: Will do well
Network	: Know who can do well

QUESTIONS TO PONDER:

1. What is hidden strength?
2. Why is developing strength a better deal?
3. Does strength mean more work? Why?

ELIMINATE WEAKNESSES

Make weaknesses irrelevant
Remove errors

Notes:
No performer is perfect. Like strengths, weaknesses exist naturally. Correcting and improving weaknesses is necessary as long as the weaknesses are in the way of performance. If they are not relevant, e.g. singing skills to a pilot, then there is no weakness to talk about. Therefore it is more strategic to eliminate weaknesses:

	Weaknesses
Skills	: Cannot do well
Attitude	: Will not do well
Network	: Don't know who can do well

QUESTIONS TO PONDER:
1. How would you define weaknesses?
2. In what ways can you remove weaknesses by job design?
3. How far are you willing to correct and improve weaknesses?

CAREER MANAGEMENT
– TOUGHEN UP

Can reach?

Notes:

Career moves are actual & realistic ways to develop the performer. To toughen him up, you can give:

	Toughen up
Projects	: More difficult things to accomplish
Customer Management Initiatives	: Handle customers directly
Change Activities	: Change status quo
Goals & Targets	: Achieve higher goals & targets

QUESTIONS TO PONDER:

1. Do you wait for performer to be ready before you toughen him up? Why?
2. How much risks are you willing to take?
3. How to balance support to give and degree of difficulty of assignments?

CAREER MANAGEMENT
– OPEN UP

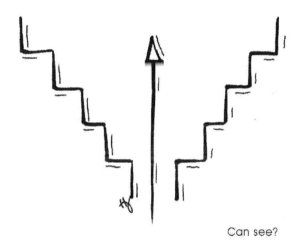

Can see?

Notes:
Career moves are actual & realistic ways to develop the performer. To open him up, you can give:

	Open up
New Assignment	: Different things to do
Different Environment	: Do it in another environment
Different Roles	: Handle new responsibilities
External Parties Liaison	: Communicate with outside people

QUESTIONS TO PONDER:
1. Do you wait for performer to be ready before you open him up? Why?
2. How much risks are you willing to take?
3. How much to open up for each time?

CAREER MANAGEMENT
– GROW UP

Can step up?

Notes:
Career moves are actual & realistic ways to develop the performer. To grow him up, you can give:

	Grow up
Higher Responsibilities	: Set directions that affect others directly
Decision Making Roles	: Make decisions that affect other's work directly
Advisory Roles	: Stay close to decision makers
Promotion	: Take charge

QUESTIONS TO PONDER:
1. Do you wait for performer to be ready before you grow him up? Why?
2. How much risks are you willing to take?
3. How can you recognize that the performer has "grown up"?

Engage Performer's Capabilities

Engage Performer's Capabilities

Engaging the performer's capabilities is a natural and logical follow up from performer's development activities. While development activities seek to improve, correct or enhance the performer, engagement activities seek to test him or her in actual work situations.

During engagement, the two aspects of technical know-how and behavioral strengths are intertwined when you see the performer in actions. The combination of expert skills with soft skills (e.g. thinking) will create the performance results that thrill and surprise every observer. The more you are aware of the required technical expertise and desired behavioral strengths, the more you can engage the performer for positive results.

The 13 ideas here are:

- Performer's capabilities
- Technical expertise (suitability)
- Technical expertise – right
- Technical expertise – effective
- Technical expertise – relevant
- Behavioral strengths (compatibility)
- Behavioral strengths – motivating
- Behavioral strengths – connecting
- Behavioral strengths – driving
- Performer's commitment – belief
- Performer's commitment – passion
- Performer's commitment – will
- Finding a performance purpose

PERFORMER'S CAPABILITIES

Coconut "Capacity"

"Stimuli"
sea

Technical expertise & behavioral strengths...
... in use

Notes:

Capability produces the decision you make & the actions you take. They are 2 important areas:

Technical expertise   : Content knowledge & process

Behavioral strengths   : Thinking & social skills, e.g. behavioral competencies

QUESTIONS TO PONDER:

1. Would your technical expertise be enough to get the job done?
2. How much success can your behavioral strengths bring for you?
3. How to tell technical expertise and behavioral strengths apart?

TECHNICAL EXPERTISE
(SUITABILITY)

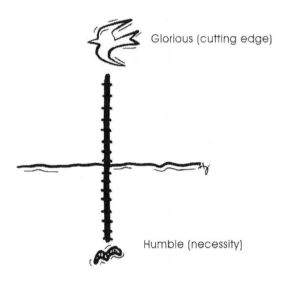

Glorious (cutting edge)

Humble (necessity)

Notes:
Technical expertise creates an expert in you. But it also covers the essential basics:

Technical expertise

Cutting edge / high specialization : Suitable to handle advanced or specialized operations

Basic job / necessity : Suitable to handle basic operations

QUESTIONS TO PONDER:
1. Would you hire someone without the needed technical expertise? Why?
2. What kind of training would you give for one who lacks technical expertise?
3. How far would you go with someone without technical expertise?

Perform! *The illustrated thoughts* by Toh Tiong Yau

TECHNICAL EXPERTISE
– RIGHT

Design for it (functionality)

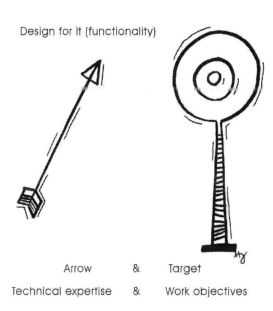

Arrow	&	Target
Technical expertise	&	Work objectives

Notes:
One with the technical expertise is the right person to do the job:

Right

Functionality   : Apply right knowledge & skills to the job

TECHNICAL EXPERTISE
– EFFECTIVE

Get the results (predictability)

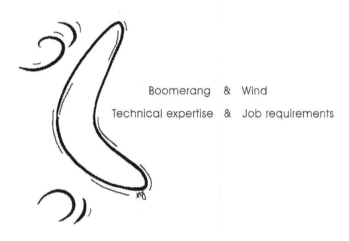

Boomerang & Wind

Technical expertise & Job requirements

Notes:
One with the technical expertise is the effective person to do the job:

Effective

Predictability   : Get the expected outcomes from the expert actions

QUESTIONS TO PONDER:
1. What can affect the effectiveness of the expert?
2. What is the error margin you can live with?
3. How to create reliability into effectiveness?

TECHNICAL EXPERTISE
– RELEVANT

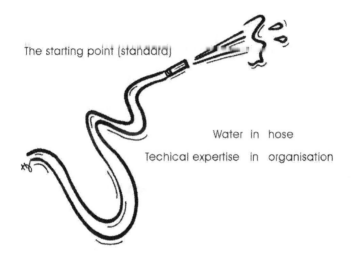

The starting point (standard)

Water in hose
Techical expertise in organisation

Notes:
One with the technical expertise is the relevant person to do the job:

Relevant

Standard : Set the standard of results to follow

BEHAVIORAL STRENGTHS
(COMPATIBILITY)

Is there attraction?

Notes:
Behavioral strengths keep you in the real world. It bonds and relates:

	Behavioral strengths
Shared values	: Compatible in ideas
Affinity	: Compatible in interests
Mutual trust	: Compatible in relationships
Mutual respect	: Compatible when in doubt

QUESTIONS TO PONDER:
1. How easy to mistake someone with behavioral strengths as having technical expertise?
2. How much can behavioral strengths compensate for a lack of technical expertise?
3. How far would you go with someone without behavioral strengths?

BEHAVIORAL STRENGTHS
– MOTIVATING

Engage the emotions (optimism)

Choice of thoughts

Choice of words

Notes:
One who possesses & uses behavioral strengths is motivating to work with:

	Motivating
Emotions	: Engage the emotions

QUESTIONS TO PONDER:
1. How can emotions make a difference at work?
2. How you think and what you say... how does it matter?
3. When can you engage someone who can motivate the rest?

BEHAVIORAL STRENGTHS
– CONNECTING

Engage the people (social)

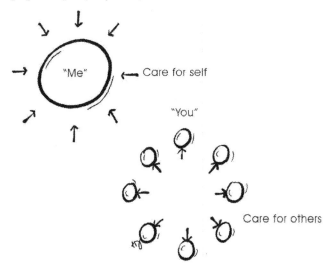

Notes:
One who possesses & uses behavioral strengths connects well with others:

Connecting

Social   : Engage the people

Perform! *The illustrated thoughts* by Toh Tiong Yau

BEHAVIORAL STRENGTHS
– DRIVING

Engage the cause (energy)

All the way?

Notes:
One who possesses & uses behavioral strengths drive the results:

Driving

Energy   : Engage the cause (common goals)

QUESTIONS TO PONDER:
1. What is work without an aim?
2. What actions would follow a constructive or destructive cause?
3. Are you driving towards something you value?

PERFORMER'S COMMITMENT
– BELIEF

Black   Grey   White

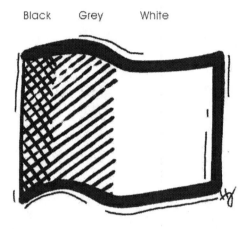

Belief : Values

Notes:
Your personal belief is absolutely true to you. It is what you value & therefore what you will commit to it:

White   : Absolutely right

Black   : Absolutely wrong

Shades of grey : Conditions for right & wrong

QUESTIONS TO PONDER:
1. Why do you commit to something that you strongly believe in?
2. How much room do you have for others to be different from you?
3. To what extent can you commit with others who differ from you?

PERFORMER'S COMMITMENT
– PASSION

Passion : Energy

Notes:
Your passion is why you cannot stop until you get what you passionately want. It is the energy of your commitment:

High points : High energy, get going

Low points : Low energy, rest to start again

QUESTIONS TO PONDER:
1. How do you prove your passion at work?
2. When nobody is interested, do you redefine your passion?
3. How can you ride on (tap on) other's passion?

PERFORMER'S COMMITMENT
– WILL

Will : Resilience

Notes:
Your will to persist shows how far you will go. It shows the resilience in holding up your commitment:

Good times   : As planned & expected

Bad times   : Everything wrong happens

QUESTIONS TO PONDER:
1. What happens to your commitment when you are forced to abandon?
2. How long would you stand alone for your own cause?
3. When will you begin to doubt?

FINDING A PERFORMANCE PURPOSE

Contributions that...

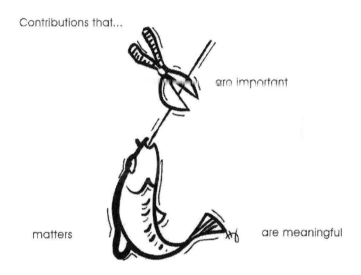

are important

matters

are meaningful

Notes:

The purpose to perform explains why you should continue.

Performance purpose

Important	: It is critical (e.g. save a life)
Meaningful	: It is what everyone wants (e.g. happy ending)
Matters	: It makes a difference (e.g. it works)

Make up your mind (M factors)

Make up your mind (M factors)

How you define yourself and what you want to achieve begin in your mind. The directions you set, the outcome you visualize or the targets you aim are examples of the first point of performance excellence.

Whether you are self initiated or prompted, conscious or not so conscious about your plan, you imagine your success before you attain it.

Your environment may or may not be conducive; your current capabilities may or may not be ready, but what mind you make up will determine the things you do next.

The 2 ideas here are:

- Stretch your goals
- Think extension

STRETCHED YOUR GOALS

How far?

Notes:
Stretched goals are like vitamins. They strengthen you and you will never be the same again.

Customers   : e.g. make them loyal

Supervising managers : e.g. make them impress

Self   : e.g. make self satisfied

Competitors   : e.g. make them re-plan

QUESTIONS TO PONDER:
1. Given existing targets, how much more can you give?
2. What is stopping you from going further?
3. Would the benefits fall short of the trouble to go further, even in longer term?

THINK EXTENSION

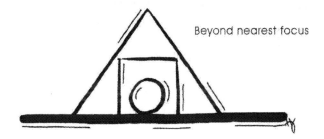

Beyond nearest focus

Notes:
Extension of outcome means going beyond present time to consider how future will be when current goals are attained. Consider what will be when now is done:

Customers   : Shift out or buy more

Supervising managers : Notice or dismiss

Self   : No change or for the better

Competitors   : Challenge or be challenged

QUESTIONS TO PONDER:
1. Why is it important to see further than now?
2. Would it make any difference since no one can predict the future? Why?
3. How useful is imagination (of what is to be) as compared to waiting to go into the future?

Power up your chances (P factors)

Power up your chances (P factors)

Before you can realize your plan, you need to act on it competently.

Every decision you make and action you take is a demonstration of your strengths and weaknesses. While strengths give you progress, weaknesses drag you behind. It is important to move forward and not lag behind. For this, working on strengths and overcoming weaknesses is a package deal.

The 2 ideas here are:

- Let your strengths count
- Make your weaknesses irrelevant

LET YOUR STRENGTHS COUNT

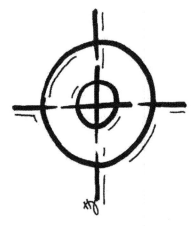

Spot the right thing to do

Notes:

Your strengths will make you contribute that in turn defines you further. Work with strengths:

Technical expertise   : What you know, technically speaking

Behavioral strengths   : What you can accomplish, especially socially

QUESTIONS TO PONDER:

1. Do you take a lot of effort just to accomplish a little? Why?
2. Do you enjoy your work now? Why?
3. How long will you stay doing your current work? Why?

MAKE YOUR WEAKNESSES IRRELEVENT

Throw

Notes:
Your weaknesses are why you fail. Be frank about them:

Technical expertise   : Level of proficiency / frequency & types of mistakes

Behavioral strengths   : Level of credibility / amount of resistances received

QUESTIONS TO PONDER:
1. How updated are you on your work?
2. In what ways are you confident about work?
3. Would you rather do something else? Why not?

Clear the air (C factors)

Clear the air (C factors)

As you never work with only bare hands and in total isolation, you would need resources and support from many others to attain your success.

The more we can benefit from what is given to us and tap on what is accessible, the more we strengthen our raw capabilities. Similarly, the quicker we realize how others can support us, the sooner we will work well with them to compensate for the skills we lack but need. This is the passport to success.

The 2 ideas here are:

- Engage what are given
- Leverage on other's gifts

ENGAGE WHAT ARE GIVEN

What else can it be used for?

Notes:

You are given things to accomplish your work. It is how conscious you are about them:

Given

Time	: It is always there
Information	: It is how selective you are
Resources	: It is the trade off
Support	: It is the give & take
Opportunity	: It is the costs you can bear

QUESTIONS TO PONDER:

1. What are things that are given to you verbally, physically & socially?
2. What are different things that you can do with what is already given?
3. How can you create new value from old stuff?

LEVERAGE ON OTHER'S GIFTS

Do more than what you can

Notes:
You are never alone at work. There are other people's gifts & strengths that are waiting for you to engage:

Other people's strengths

Knowledge	: What is right & wrong
Experience	: What will work & won't work
Network	: Who else can help
Resources	: What can be "borrowed"
Time	: What can be outsourced

QUESTIONS TO PONDER:
1. Who else can make you better at work? (What strengths do they bring to you?)
2. How can you cooperate with them that you have not so far?
3. What kind of win-win propositions can you initiate?